A Day at the Beach.

A seaside counting book relating numerals, words and objects for young readers.

One fisherman on the beach.

Two girls playing in the sand.

Three pails waiting to be filled.

Four sandcastles, watch out for waves!

Five sailboats racing.

Six crabs playing hide and seek.

Seven dolphins frolicking in the surf.

Eight wiggly octopus **legs.**

Nine shimmering seashells.

10

Ten hungry seagulls looking for lunch.

Find and point to:

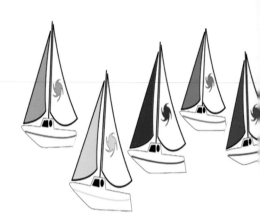

1. One fisherman.

2. Two girls.

3. Three pails.

4. Four sandcastles.

 5. Five sailboats.

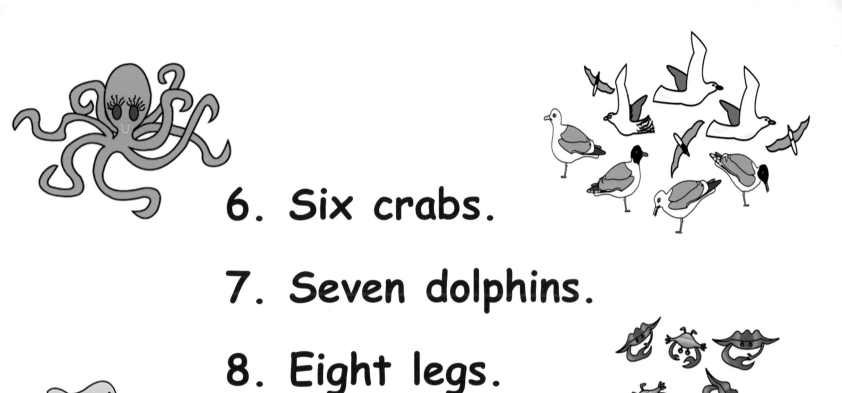

6. Six crabs.

7. Seven dolphins.

8. Eight legs.

9. Nine seashells.

10. Ten seagulls.

What would you play with if you were on this beach?